TheBlackM

MW01249103

Define Yourself, Redefine the World

A Guided Journal for Boys and Men of Color
Edition 2

Created by Brandon Frame

CreateSpace
South Carolina

Edited by Literacy Lives LLC.
JoVonna Rodriguez

Cover Design by Julian Streete

Copyright © 2014 by TheBlackManCan; Brandon Frame

ISBN-13: 978-1505708189

ISBN-10: 1505708184

This journal belongs to:

_____

Table of Contents

Dear Journalist,

This journal is for you. Designed to motivate, inspire, and enlighten. Every page includes an encouraging and informative quote from a man of color in progress. Space is provided for you to write down your thoughts and answer essential questions to help you plan your future.

Now is the time for you to start thinking about the choices you've made and will make. Now is the time to take the necessary steps to ensure that you become an upstanding young man. As males, we often hold thoughts and emotions deep inside of our hearts. It is customary for us to harbor our emotions and feelings inside, deciding against expressing them to anyone. We usually do not invest the time it takes to effectively communicate with others, or most importantly, ourselves.

I decided to create this journal for us, men of color. It's vital that we create outlets to uplift and educate one another. We must be supportive and encouraging because the true strength to conquer life lies within you. The quotes and essential questions were chosen to make you think critically about relevant topics on your road to being the best man you can be. It's essential that you aim for greatness for yourself, family, and society at large.

"Define Yourself, Redefine the World," is more than just a title; it's an actual feeling that I want you to internalize. As you answer the essential questions throughout this journal understand this: the more you are aware of yourself, the easier it becomes to have a meaningful impact on others. It is my hope that this journal will assist you on your path to defining yourself.

It's imperative to define yourself as the man you aim to be. Through such definition, you are able to redefine the world. The world needs you to harness your full potential so you can make measureable contributions to society and create tremendous change. Take all of the questions seriously because they are meant to shape and build your critical consciousness. The world needs you to show up in the most vibrant and authentic way possible. Now go write and remember to "Be Different, Be Great, Never Stop!"

Brandon Frame
Chief Visionary Officer
TheBlackManCan

Pledge

I will live my life as the wonderful creation I am.

I will coat my mind with knowledge so it will not be penetrated by foolishness.

I will value brotherhood and will always be my brother's keeper.

My stride is wide because I walk in the footsteps of giants.

I will define myself so I can redefine the world.

I will be different, I will be great, I will never stop!

Education

"Education is the key to success."

We hear that phrase a lot, but what does it really mean?

Self-knowledge is education. Learning how to be organized, disciplined, articulate, and responsible for your growth encompasses education. Complete control for the information that enters your being is education. Being accountable for what you teach others is education.

Education is the key that opens doors in life. Your ability to find the positive in the negative, to persevere, to be knowledgeable, to debate, argue, speak for yourself, stand for what's right, and most importantly, changing your life and others is all based on the education you receive.

Understand that education and knowledge does not start or stop with schooling. You have the power to be enlightened in and outside of the classroom. Challenge yourself and others. Change yourself and others, by starting with the things you learn. Remember no one can steal the knowledge you possess, protect and value it. Use this next session to plan your educational success, document your knowledge, and explore new things.

Make education your hustle. If you are truly educated, you get access to opportunities and resources that many will not receive.
~ Dr. Walter Kimbrough

You can always tell a good educator by the way students act around he or she outside of the classroom. ~ Eric Tillman

When students have a bond with you it's like a soul-tie; they trust you to never lead them wrong or misuse their trust. Because we are human we all make mistakes but a student can still trust you for who you are. ~ Eric Tillman

_____
_____
_____
_____
_____
_____
_____
_____
_____
_____
_____
_____
_____
_____
_____
_____
_____
_____
_____
_____
_____
_____
_____
_____
_____
_____
_____
_____

Reading books has always been a part of my life.
~ Dennis R. Upkins

_____

_____

_____

_____

_____

_____

_____

_____

_____

_____

_____

_____

_____

_____

_____

_____

_____

_____

_____

_____

_____

_____

_____

_____

_____

_____

_____

_____

_____

_____

When students are having fun in class, they will be learning at the same time without even realizing they are learning. ~ Darryl Baynes

Essential Question #1

What does education mean to you? What is the difference between book smarts and street smarts? How do these play a role in your life?

_____

_____

_____

_____

_____

_____

_____

_____

_____

_____

_____

_____

_____

_____

_____

_____

_____

_____

_____

_____

_____

_____

_____

_____

_____

_____

_____

_____

_____

_____

We must learn, and never stop learning the things that will provide us the means to live a life and provide opportunities for others to live theirs. ~ Charles H.F. Davis

I feel there are many voids that need to be filled, but by tapping into the creativity of youth gives them the positive spark that they will need to succeed in today's competitive society. ~ Matthew Smith

You'd be surprised what reading can do for your vocabulary and your overall approach towards words. ~ Kel Spencer

No matter what, with an education the market value of you as a person is even better. ~ Marcus Singletary

_____

_____

_____

_____

_____

_____

_____

_____

_____

_____

_____

_____

_____

_____

_____

_____

_____

_____

_____

_____

_____

_____

_____

_____

_____

_____

_____

_____

_____

_____

_____

Write correctly, speak correctly and don't be afraid to be smart. Let you imagination run wild. ~ Vensin Gray

Essential Question

How will you take control over the knowledge you learn and share?

_____

_____

_____

_____

_____

_____

_____

_____

_____

_____

_____

_____

_____

_____

_____

_____

_____

_____

_____

_____

_____

_____

_____

_____

_____

_____

The only way to break a negative cycle is to become educated.
~ Orayne Williams

_____

_____

_____

_____

_____

_____

_____

_____

_____

_____

_____

_____

_____

_____

_____

_____

_____

_____

_____

_____

_____

_____

_____

_____

_____

_____

What does matter now is just being yourself and how well you prepare yourself through education for the future. ~ Mike Mose

_____
_____
_____
_____
_____
_____
_____
_____
_____
_____
_____
_____
_____
_____
_____
_____
_____
_____
_____
_____
_____
_____
_____
_____
_____
_____
_____
_____
_____
_____

How can we change our trajectory in life if we don't get the
information to do so? ~ Terrell Hill

I believe that students who are focused and passionate about what they are studying, do better. ~ Terrell Hill

_____

_____

_____

_____

_____

_____

_____

_____

_____

_____

_____

_____

_____

_____

_____

_____

_____

_____

_____

_____

_____

_____

_____

_____

_____

_____

Educate yourself with as much knowledge as possible.
Knowledge is self-empowerment and, to a certain degree, brings
freedom. ~ Keishorne Scott

Essential Question #3

What are your needs in order to be a better learner? How can others help you with these needs? How can you start helping yourself?

_____

_____

_____

_____

_____

_____

_____

_____

_____

_____

_____

_____

_____

_____

_____

_____

_____

_____

_____

_____

_____

_____

_____

_____

_____

_____

_____

_____

Enjoy your time as students. As annoying as it may be, it's the last time in your life when you won't have to worry about where the food is coming from or where you will sleep. ~Akil Bello

I'm still learning on a daily basis and working to master my craft.
~ Brother Jesse Muhammad

One message I always drive home is the true purpose of education, having a purpose in life and living a meaningful life that enhances and touches the lives of others. ~ Brother Jesse Muhammad

Get as much formal education and training as you can, get involved in your community; what you do today will help determine the kind of world we will have tomorrow. ~ Mayor Wayne Smith

Once you make the decision to be a continuous learner, you make the decision for your opportunities to be limitless. Your thirst for knowledge must be like that of a man in the desert for weeks without a thought of water! ~ Alfred Blake

Essential Question #4

What do you need from your parents, siblings, community, and mentors in order to excel with school and education?

_____

_____

_____

_____

_____

_____

_____

_____

_____

_____

_____

_____

_____

_____

_____

_____

_____

_____

_____

_____

_____

_____

_____

_____

_____

_____

The foundation of my academic success was the ability to manage my time. ~ L. Trenton Marsh

_____

_____
_____
_____
_____
_____
_____
_____
_____
_____
_____
_____
_____
_____
_____
_____
_____
_____
_____
_____
_____
_____
_____
_____
_____
_____
_____
_____
_____
_____
_____
_____

Spiritual

The concept of having faith is the ability to have trust or confidence in something or someone. In a spiritual sense, faith is backed by your belief and trust in a Higher Power. Everything serves a purpose in life, and sometimes we cannot see or understand everything in a physical sense. It's important to develop your own personal concept of faith and hope in order to find purpose and value in your life.

In times of joy you can celebrate your blessings. Hope brought you through in order to reap rewards. In times of stress, hope keeps you focused while faith decreases your worry. How you think about this determines how you act. It increases your gratitude and you learn how to appreciate the small things in life. Give praise for waking up every day and having the strength to get through each day.

Take the time to question spirituality. Develop a personal relationship with your Higher Power that suits your reality and desires. Lean on your faith to provide stability in this world of uncertainty we live in. Bring hope to every situation you face. Look for positivity at all times. Start today.

It is my responsibility to take the gifts that God has given me to make a difference in the world where I can. ~ Darryl Baynes

I believe a spiritual foundation in God is important because it provides a focus outside of our own perspective. ~ Kenny Pugh

Because God is limitless and no eye nor ear has seen or heard the limit to HIS power, and I know that power runs through me-changing the world will not be a problem. ~ Eric Tillman

Know what you have stacked against you and be so hungry with your faith in God that no weapon formed against you can prosper.
~ Eric Tillman

My advice, life will knock you down, don't allow that experience to knock you out. God has placed a spirit of excellence over your life. Go forth and live a life that matters. ~ Ricardo P. Deveaux

Essential Question #1

Do you believe in a higher spiritual power?

Always believe in yourself, always dream big, and always stay
connected to the main source. ~ Marcus Singletary

God is amazing. He saved my life, why can't he save yours?
Always believe. ~ Omarr Lee

Building a spiritual foundation is very essential to anyone's overall growth in life. ~ Omarr Lee

_____

_____

_____

_____

_____

_____

_____

_____

_____

_____

_____

_____

_____

_____

_____

_____

_____

_____

_____

_____

_____

_____

_____

_____

_____

_____

_____

_____

_____

_____

Stay encouraged. Life may seem like it's taking a toll on you but God can sustain you in the midst of trouble. ~ J. Newry

Everything that is tangible in life can be stripped away from you. But your belief in God, and education can never be taken away. You must increase both consistently. ~ Cenell Harrell

Essential Question #2

What does faith mean to you?

_____

_____

_____

_____

_____

_____

_____

_____

_____

_____

_____

_____

_____

_____

_____

_____

_____

_____

_____

_____

_____

_____

_____

_____

_____

A *Dream Catalyst* is one who provides ideas, insights, and inspiration to others to help them activate their dreams and pursue their life purpose. I am passionate and committed to doing this for others because I want to see people live up to their God-given potential. ~ Paul Wilson, Jr.

_____

_____

_____

_____

_____

_____

_____

_____

_____

_____

_____

_____

_____

_____

_____

_____

_____

_____

_____

_____

_____

_____

_____

_____

_____

Be sure to always take care of yourself health wise and fellowship with God. Have a respectful and appreciative relationship with parents and adults that cross your path. ~ Marcus Singletary

Too many times in our culture we are taught independence and self-sufficiency and not dependency upon our faith. ~ Andre Knighton

_____

_____

_____

_____

_____

_____

_____

_____

_____

_____

_____

_____

_____

_____

_____

_____

_____

_____

_____

_____

_____

_____

_____

_____

_____

_____

_____

Adversity isn't necessarily a horrible thing. It's an uncomfortable thing. I believe God talks to all of us through not only positive situations, but also the bad ones as well. ~ Alan Hamilton

Adversity forces us to learn about ourselves, it's what we do with that education that determines whether we are victims or victorious for having gone through the experience. ~ Alan Hamilton

Essential Question #3

Describe a time when you faced a challenge and used faith or hope to guide you through.

Know that where you are isn't where you HAVE to be. We can create the destinies we desire. We can be the change in the world we want to see. ~ Fahamu Pecou

Obstacles are only tests of character and will. ~ Wesley Bellamy

Through hard work and faith you can achieve anything that your mind can conceptualize. ~ Alan Hamilton

For without tests in life, I would not know how to trust God and understand that in due time, all storms cease, and the sun will shine.
~ Wesley Bellamy

Create like a god. Command like a king. Work like a slave.
~ Fahamu Pecou

Essential Question #4

Having faith helps put the mind at ease and minimize worry. When you are stressed out what will be your plan of action to decrease your worry?

_____

_____

_____

_____

_____

_____

_____

_____

_____

_____

_____

_____

_____

_____

_____

_____

_____

_____

_____

_____

_____

_____

_____

_____

_____

Have faith and believe that you can and will prevail in the end, regardless of difficulties. Additionally, have the discipline and courage to confront the most brutal facts of your current reality, whatever they might be. ~ Wesley Bellamy

Career Advice

So many adults spend the later years of their lives chasing their childhood dreams, goals, and passions. You have the chance not to make the mistake of waiting. Don't hesitate to chase your dreams now. Don't put your goals on a list that you will never revisit. Most importantly, learn to invest in your passions.

The best job is the one you're excited to wake up for, go to, and would often do for free. You might ask why, and the answer is that it's truly a job that you love. A job that you're so great at that it seems effortless. A career that gives you fulfillment and a sense of accomplishment with every step. Chase after this feeling, put your passions to good use, and make a career out of them.

How do you do this? Think about all the things you are great at doing. Think about services that you can offer friends, family, strangers, and your community that you would love to do. Think about what your ideal job would be. Take the time in this next section to use this space to build on those thoughts, write down your visions, and plan your next steps.

My advice to anyone looking to start a business would be to love what you do, embrace change, and get educated on basic business principles like accounting, management, and marketing; or partner with people who are strong in those areas. ~ Julian Streete

I encourage boys and men of color to pursue the area of life they truly enjoy and would do full-time if compensation, power, or failure weren't potential obstacles. ~ Kenny Pugh

Find someone to mentor you and be a mentor to others. If at anytime your journey towards your future success stops being fun, pause, and figure out a way to make it fun again. ~ Al Coleman, Jr.

My advice to an aspiring photographer: Be a photographer. Don't be a Guy with a Camera (GWC). Learn the craft of photography. Then when you think you know it all, go back, and learn some more.
~ Ivory Lawrence

No one knows it all. There's a thousand ways to do everything but the one constant is that you have to know what you are doing to the point where you can develop your own way of doing it.
~ Ivory Lawrence

Essential Question #1

What is your dream career and why?

Everyone has talents and should have a business to earn additional income off their talents. ~ Orayne Williams

---

Acting is my life. I'm illiterate without it. Acting has taught me how to value patience and rejection. ~ Jarret Janako

As we lead our lives, it is imperative that we keep in mind the spirit of Rosa Parks- a woman who has received a countless number of awards and honors. However, she isn't remembered for what she received, but for what she has given. ~ David McGhee

Hard work is simple, you have to put in the work to reap the results or else you will just be average. ~ Marcus Singletary

Never become complacent with your position in life because that is not what is meant for you. ~ Marcus Singletary

Essential Question #2

What will you do to make sure that you have your dream career?

You never know who may give you a chance to show your talent or skill. You never know who may give you the opportunity to have your movie made. You never know who is listening to your heart because dreaming is an art from the heart. ~ Omarr Lee

Developing good habits of setting objectives, creating a timeline, and following through, will benefit you tremendously in life.
~ Akil Bello

Success is what you do to achieve your goals. Significance is what you do to equip, motivate, and position others to achieve their goals. If we chase success, we may never get significance. If we chase significance, we'll pass success along the way. ~ Paul Wilson, Jr.

The time that I spent in corporate provided me with the training and development needed for my entrepreneurial success. It is through my corporate experiences where the professional development has occurred. ~ Alvin Perry

In order to reach a certain level of success in life you have to be willing to respond differently to adversity and do things other people are not willing to do. ~ Kenny Pugh

Essential Question #3

What are your strengths?

_____
_____
_____
_____
_____
_____
_____
_____
_____
_____
_____
_____
_____
_____
_____
_____
_____
_____
_____
_____
_____
_____
_____
_____
_____
_____
_____
_____

A committed mindset, undying will, faith, and fortitude, gave me the
strength to overcome the odds and obstacles in life.
~ Eddie Connor, Jr.

When we truly understand who we are, including our personality, passions, and professional skills, we can better align our calling with our career choices. ~ Paul Wilson, Jr.

Strive for greatness and don't let anyone convince you that you aren't worthy or you can't do it. ~ Dennis Upkins

Don't STOP. Keep going. Keep growing. Keep living. God first and everything else is everything else. ~ Brandon McEachern

Never be afraid to share what is in your heart. I suggest you journal your thoughts and feelings. ~ Pervis Taylor, III

Essential Question #4

What are your favorite things to do? How can you turn them into services?

_____

_____

_____

_____

_____

_____

_____

_____

_____

_____

_____

_____

_____

_____

_____

_____

_____

_____

_____

_____

_____

_____

_____

_____

_____

Life isn't about getting secured with just a job, it's about living a meaningful life—one that touches and enhances the lives of others.
~ Brother Jesse Muhammad

Advice to Young Men of Color

We all face challenges in life that can wear us down. Sometimes it is our inner strength that gets us through. Sometimes it is our support system that lifts us up. Sometimes it is the advice from others that helps us make better decisions.

Remember, in your times of need that there are men before you and will be young men after you who have or will have gone through similar situations. Don't be afraid to speak up about your feelings, circumstances, goals, and needs. Don't put your progression on hold waiting on others to help you.

Look to those who came before you as strength to push forward. Look to the mistakes of others to serve as examples of what not to do. Study the lives of greatness in order to make your life full of it as well.

Know that you're not alone on this road called Life. There are strong Men of Color leading the way. There are strong Men of Color who came before you. Know that you're of greatness and can achieve anything you desire.

As an older male of color you have to have the bold courage to tell them the truth. It sounds better coming from one that was either focusing solely on making it and did not or one that made it and then messed up because of lack of education. ~ Eric Tillman

Advice to young boys of color: I get it. We get it. We get the pain you endure that you're not allowed to acknowledge. We get the hardships and bigotry you face that you're gaslit into being told that it's all in your head. You live in a world that assumes the worst out of you, that eagerly waits to see you fail, that looks on you suspiciously if you beat the odds and prosper. ~ Dennis R. Upkins

We hear you. You're not alone. There are those of us out there who are fighting for you, fighting to improve things. ~ Dennis R. Upkins

Be the change that you want to see in the world. Strive for greatness and don't let anyone convince you that you aren't worthy or you can't do it. Don't believe the lies. It's not easy, no, and it's a struggle, but there are many of us out here doing it every day.
~ Dennis R. Upkins

Never apologize for being a descendant of greatness and never apologize for striving to attain greatness. Whatever your goals are, stay focused on them and keep working at them. Whether or not you reach your goal, you'll certainly be further along than where you started. ~ Dennis R. Upkins

Essential Question #1

Write a letter to your future self with advice you would give someone else from the things you've experienced in life thus far.

_____

_____

_____

_____

_____

_____

_____

_____

_____

_____

_____

_____

_____

_____

_____

_____

_____

_____

_____

_____

_____

_____

_____

_____

_____

_____

_____

_____

_____

_____

_____

It takes a real man to be able to make intelligent decisions related to how not to make the same mistakes as everyone else. Your strength to say no and be a change agent may just be the one thing that causes a chain reaction of others to follow in your footsteps.

~ Christopher Small

A real man has mastered himself. ~ Tim Lee

In today's society my advice to young males is to do their best in whatever they participate in. Be involved in all the positive activities that your school offers. ~ Matt Smith

Prove them wrong. Show those outdated statistics that black men are powerful. ~ Jarret Janako

No matter what happened in the past, don't look back and never ever give up. ~ Charles H.F. Davis

Essential Question #2

Write a letter to your future self asking questions that you can't ask anyone else.

_____

_____

_____

_____

_____

_____

_____

_____

_____

_____

_____

_____

_____

_____

_____

_____

_____

_____

_____

_____

_____

_____

_____

_____

_____

A warrior is tactical, wise, brave, and physical. ~ Kel Spencer

Just be honest with yourself, and your family. Be a good person in your community. If throughout your entire life, you help one person and one person alone, then you did well for yourself.
~ Vensin Gray

Man of Color, you have to begin this day with courage in your life. You have to face each day with strength within yourself. Master your own emotions each day. Deal with your struggles and learn to overcome. You have a future. You will succeed. Don't give up.
~ John Phillip Autry, II

My advice to young boys of color is to build mental toughness. There are going to be so many obstacles and people who say that you cannot make it. Stay focused on your dreams and do not let anything stand in your way. ~ Jarrett Mathis

Be yourself. Be careful of the company that you keep. Believe what you're inspired to do. Be the best that you can possibly be. Be patient. Be persistent. Be the change that you want to see.
~ Basheer Jones

Essential Question #3

What advice would you give to your peers?

What you do in life can be the determining factor of what someone watching you will achieve. Live to BECOME the Example.
~ George Olokun

Don't let anybody put you in a box defined by his or her expectations. It's never too early to start pursuing your dreams. The impossible is possible for you when you align your passions, purpose, and giftedness with God's plan for your life.
~ Paul Wilson, Jr.

Respect yourselves, respect your culture, understand your history and protect, uplift, and support women. Pretty simple but at times extremely hard to do. ~ Renard Antonio Green

If one more educated male of color can go through the struggle and make it; then the next one can. ~ Keishorne Scott

Be yourself and help motivate and encourage each other on the path
to progress and success. ~ Mike Mose

Essential Question #4

Do you take your own advice?

A boy needs many things, however, to enter into manhood these six things are essential:

A strong identity.   A sense of gender.
A sense of self.   An awareness of his culture.
A sense of community.   A spiritual base.

~ Colbert Williams

Leadership

What does it mean to be a leader? What personality traits does a leader possess? Who are the leaders in your community? When have you acted as a leader? These are all insightful questions to keep you focused on developing leadership qualities.

Leaders speak up for what is right. Leaders are not afraid to act outside of the box. Leaders follow their dreams. Leaders take chances. Leaders motivate, inspire, and enlighten others. Leaders serve communities, donating their time and passion to help others. Leaders make wise decisions based on reflection not reaction.

Be responsible for your power. Learn how to manifest and control it. Build on your ability to be a leader in different capacities and scenarios. Use this space to critically think about what it means to be a leader. Analyze the leaders around you. What are they doing that is excellent or needs improvements? Visualize yourself as a leader, today!

My personal competitive advantages include my persistence, ability to relate to clients and audiences, and quickness to adapt to change.
~ Julian Streete

Everyone should view failure as a stepping-stone and learning opportunity towards future success. ~ Kenny Pugh

Each person must believe that they have a gift, develop that gift, and use it to better their sphere of influence. ~ Darryl Baynes

Always strive to raise your A-game. Always hone your craft. Be the best you can possibly be each day and then tomorrow be better. Do better. ~ Dennis Upkins

You must have a clear vision of what you expect to learn, how you are expected to carry yourself, and how to achieve your goals.
~ Christopher Small

Essential Question #1

What does it mean to be a great leader?

It only takes one positive male of color to make a difference.
~ Christopher Small

You are empowered to succeed in this life. There's a slot for you in history either as a world changer or someone who watched the world change. ~ Pervis Taylor, III

_____

_____

_____

_____

_____

_____

_____

_____

_____

_____

_____

_____

_____

_____

_____

_____

_____

_____

_____

_____

_____

_____

_____

_____

_____

_____

_____

_____

_____

Responsibility motivates action. ~ Tim Lee

Anyone who is really interested in helping shape the future will give much of his or her focus and attention on the upcoming generation.
~ Tim Lee

Everyone should become a mentor. We all have things we can offer others. ~ Orayne Williams

Essential Question #2

What personality traits should a leader possess?

_____

_____

_____

_____

_____

_____

_____

_____

_____

_____

_____

_____

_____

_____

_____

_____

_____

_____

_____

_____

_____

_____

_____

_____

_____

_____

_____

Having a mentor allows you to see further in every aspect of life.
Every young person should have access to be able to see further.
~ David McGhee

All that we do, all that we accomplish, and all that we believe should be for the well being and benefit of others. This is the true essence of leadership. ~ David McGhee

Beyond anything, just believe in yourself. Believe in your talents and words. You'll be amazed what you can accomplish. ~ Vensin Gray

I like when people tell me I can't make it or will not make it because then I am more determined to prove them wrong. ~ Orayne Williams

Everyone needs a support system; if it had not been for my support system I wouldn't be here today. ~ Orayne Williams

Essential Question #3

Who are the leaders in your community?

_____

_____

_____

_____

_____

_____

_____

_____

_____

_____

_____

_____

_____

_____

_____

_____

_____

_____

_____

_____

_____

_____

_____

_____

_____

You can't send a soldier to war with no weapons. You must come prepared in life. ~ Orayne Williams

Two reasons motivate me to give back, our fallen ancestors and the future generations. ~ Howard R. Jean

_____

_____

_____

_____

_____

_____

_____

_____

_____

_____

_____

_____

_____

_____

_____

_____

_____

_____

_____

_____

_____

_____

_____

_____

_____

_____

Legacy building through legacy giving is something I feel that we all should take part in. ~ Howard R. Jean

It's important that people see successful examples of Men of Color in their homes, schools, churches, and in their community.
~ Dr. Raymond Hicks

Everyone who aspires will not achieve his or her goal. Those who do, work toward that goal by being excellent at every step, rather than just worrying about the end goal. ~ Dr. Walter Kimbrough

Essential Question #4

What are you doing to ensure you continue to grow and develop as a leader?

_____

_____

_____

_____

_____

_____

_____

_____

_____

_____

_____

_____

_____

_____

_____

_____

_____

_____

_____

_____

_____

_____

_____

Your strength to say no and be a change agent may just be the one thing that causes a chain reaction of others to follow in your footsteps. ~ Chris Small

Building Your Passions, & Finding Your Purpose

Sometimes we find ourselves wondering why we're here and what we're supposed to do while we figure this out. For some of us, this is clearly defined by our skill(s) or by a family trade. Some of us have a knack for everything. Some of us will take our entire lives to comprehend our purposes and the meaning behind our lives. So what are we to do in the meantime? Do what you love and love what you do. Be full of encouragement and possibility. Don't dwell on the fact that you can't do certain things; but, marvel in your abilities to do something else! Find value and meaning in all that you do. If you give your actions purpose, you give your life purpose.

Don't be afraid to step out into a world full of possibility and creativity--even in the midst of naysayers. Don't hesitate to celebrate your strengths, highlight your successes, and congratulate yourself from time to time. Most importantly, don't be afraid of failure. Failure is the best thing that can happen to you. Learn from failure. Learn from trying. Try again and perfect trying until you succeed. The only failure is the attempt you don't make.

Once you are used to acknowledging all that you have to offer to yourself, you can see what you offer to friends, family, and the world. Evaluate what your heart desires. Try to define your strengths and ways to monetize them or use them for the greater good. Find value in everything you touch, say, and do. Be about action. Embody your passions. Step outside the box and chase your purpose.

Continue dreaming BIG dreams.
Whatever you desire to become IS a possibility if you work hard,
learn from your journey, surround yourself with positive people, and
make up in your mind to NEVER quit. ~ Kenny Pugh

Dream big dreams and set your expectations high. A successful life is not the end goal, but rather a lifelong journey. ~ Darryl Baynes

Success comes daily. ~ Pervis Taylor, III

A wise person once told me that,
"The greatest threat to your future achievements are you past accomplishments." ~ Al Coleman, Jr.

My advice would be not to rush life, take it as it comes. Prepare yourself for the future and keep in mind anything worth having takes hard work. ~ LaVar Young

Essential Question #1

Identify five of your passions. How you can put each one into action for a greater purpose?

The more you have to offer, the more appealing you are. You have to be realistic about your journey and give yourself a timetable for your goals. Nothing happens overnight. ~ LaVar Young

You have no excuse for making whatever dream you have come true. We come from people who fulfilled their dreams from nothing.
~ Darryl Frierson

I decided not to be a person who complained about the problem but one who became a part of the solution. ~ Mike Mose

Nothing in life with value comes easy. You have to work hard to realize and fulfill your dreams. Question everything. Just because someone says something that you may not like or that doesn't make you feel good, think before responding. Ask yourself if the comment can help you grow as a person? ~ Terrell Hill

At the core of everyone lives a dream, purpose, and mission in life. That dream, purpose, and mission has to be managed like a company and taken seriously as if it is worth millions of dollars.
~ Howard R. Jean

Essential Question #2

If failure is not an option, what would you do?

The worst situation brought out the best in me, so now I can use my testimony to bless and bring out the best in others.
~ Eddie Connor, Jr.

The FIRE that burns from within serves as a driving force for your success; so if you allow others to blow your fire out, don't wonder why you are not successful. ~ George Olokun

Soul searching is the catalyst. ~ Karl-Edwin Guerre

Don't be afraid to try something outside of your comfort zone. Listen to advice, but most importantly listen to yourself. Finally, dream big and strive to be the best. ~ J.T. Solomon

You must be DRIVEN to succeed at anything in life. DRIVEN is simply defined as having constant movement towards your destination. Remember, inertia is the silent assassin of all dreams and goals. ~ Cenell Harrell

Essential Question #3

How do you stay motivated to carry out your purpose?

You must maximize your talents with dedication, perseverance, and a work ethic second to none. ~ Kevin Ollie

Create a priority agenda, timeline, and assertive personality.
~ Mayor Wayne Smith

In short, people aren't looking for the causes or explanations for their problems—they are looking for solutions. ~ Tim Lee

We all want to go from nothing to something and there is a process and journey that comes along with it. ~ Darryl Frierson

The discovery of personal progression is fueled by the cycle of refreshing obstacles in life, which lead us into a state of mind where the realization that forward motion begins with self-motivation.
~ George Olokun

Essential Question #4

What do you want your legacy to be?

Don't chase nightmares, chase dreams. ~ Jarret Janako

Words of Wisdom

A wise man is stronger than any insult, tragedy, or struggle that is put upon him. Learning how to slowly respond with detail, strategy, and purpose is a sign of wisdom. Watch your speech and movements, instead be still and listen. Being humble, compassionate, firm, focused, fearless, and resilient are character traits of a wise human being.

Everything that your elders tell you may not make sense now. But soon, in the near future as you experience life, everything will fall into place. Words will replay, situations will reappear, and advice and memories will serve as slide shows pointing you in the correct way. Be open to receiving wisdom from those worthy to give.

Coulda, shoulda, woulda only last for seconds. Once something is done it cannot be taken back. Work on becoming wise in your speech and actions so that you don't have to spend time trying to right your wrongs. Use this space to explore the concept of wisdom. Take these quotes and let them sink and lead you on your path.

"Extraordinary is my ordinary, greatness is the beginning." This quote should let you know that you MUST create what hasn't been created. You must walk tall when people try to downplay your goals and dreams. ~ Rahfeal Gordon

It's often said that your perception is your reality. Your perception grows through exposure and how you relate with others.
~ Julian Streete

Stay humble enough to remember that you're a work in progress and always strive to do better so you can be better. ~ Dennis Upkins

You have been placed on this earth not just to take up space but to
create an atmosphere of change. ~ Ricardo Deveaux

You can't begin to address weaknesses in your personal development if you don't identify them first. ~ Al Coleman, Jr.

Essential Question #1

Make a motto for yourself that would serve as inspiration for future generations.

_____

_____

_____

_____

_____

_____

_____

_____

_____

_____

_____

_____

_____

_____

_____

_____

_____

_____

_____

_____

_____

_____

_____

_____

Listen to the wisdom of elders. ~ Tim Lee

Apply truth to your life, for such action is what makes you free. Knowledge of truth is just the first step. Application is the leap of faith. ~ Tim Lee

Inferiority is learned. ~ Tim Lee

Life is not a sprint or a marathon. It is a triathlon. ~ Darryl Frierson

We go through many tasks and lessons that we have to learn. The only one who can make things happen is YOU.
~ Darryl Frierson

Essential Question #2

What advice would you give to the younger generation?

Balance is the key to life. ~ Kel Spencer

Guard your heart and always keep your nose to the grindstone.
Character is defined when no one is watching. ~ Marcus Singletary

Hunger is something that we all must have in order to make it in life.
~ Marcus Singletary

Once you figure out who you are, you will be unstoppable in your pursuit of success. ~ Orayne Williams

Passing down wealth is imperative but also passing down the virtue of giving, benefits an entire society. ~ Howard R. Jean

Essential Question #3

List the three wisest people you know. What makes them wise?

Your value is not about what you have, your true value is based upon who you are. ~ Eddie Connor, Jr.

Remember, nothing just happens. If you want different results, you have to DO something different! ~ L. Trenton Marsh

Do not downplay your greatness for the sake of making others feel comfortable around you. Shine your light and force them to step their game up! ~ Brother Jesse Muhammad

Greatness is not acquired, it is realized.
Once you realize your greatness, you can accomplish great things!
~ Alfred Blake

No one is guaranteed a life of roses or one of suffering, learn to live with both as all tides shift at some point.
~ Karl-Edwin Guerre

Essential Question #4

What mistakes have you made? What did you learn from them?

Run like a fugitive towards your goals, if you stop, you can become imprisoned by mediocrity. ~ Alfred Blake

Relationships

When we speak of relationships, often times our mind only think about romantic relationships. However, don't limit yourself to this type of thinking. The relationships we build with other individuals are just as vital as those with loved ones.

Relationships are the quilts of life. Invest in your interactions with others. You can build bonds with strangers and friends and become family. Learn the power of honesty, communication, and action. Understand the difference between personal, professional, and business relationships. Learn how to maneuver through them all with a smile and optimistic outlook.

Use this section to increase your understanding of how to deal with other people. Think about how you can be a better speaker, listener, and doer. Be proactive about the relationships that you develop from this day forward. Guard and protect whom you allow in your circle.

We have been placed here to become better husbands, fathers, sons, cousins, and mentors. ~ Ricardo P. Deveaux

_____

_____

_____

_____

_____

_____

_____

_____

_____

_____

_____

_____

_____

_____

_____

_____

_____

_____

_____

_____

_____

_____

_____

_____

_____

_____

_____

We must love our mothers, wives, daughters, and sisters; we must treat them as our *QUEENS*. ~ Ricardo P. Deveaux

Our deepest fear is not that we don't know where we are going in life but that we don't know who we are. Once we figure out who we are, we can be unstoppable in the pursuit of success.
~ Orayne Williams

Become conscious of your daily thoughts and when a negative thought enters your mind quickly turn it around. ~ Keishorne Scott

As human beings we are all predisposed to hereditary traits that are passed down by our family members. I believe that my mother passed to me dogmatic determination and the power to persevere.
~ Eddie Connor, Jr.

Essential Question #1

What is a healthy relationship? List some of the healthy relationships you have with other people.

Normally, the word "ignorant" carries a negative connotation, but what if we were ignorant to the fact that our hearts could be broken. I believe we would love more. Or, if we were ignorant to things that cause fear, judgment or rejection, I believe we would dream more.
~ James Bland

Establish healthy foundations of relationships built upon love, communication, respect, trust, and common interest. ~ Kenny Pugh

In the context of romantic relationships, a lot of people can create happiness lying down. However, the better question to ask is if a person can make you happy standing up. ~ Kenny Pugh

You're going to make a lot of mistakes. Give yourself permission to make those mistakes. Mistakes are a part of life. Don't beat yourself up. Mistakes are how we grow. ~ Colbert Williams

Boys and Men of Color not only need to be exposed to positive images of themselves, but they also need to experience ongoing healthy relationships and support from other boys and men of color. Such relationships are critical to their emotional, social, and psychological development throughout their lifespan. ~ Dr. James L. Moore, III

Essential Question #2

Make a list of all the important factors that help you develop healthy relationships.

_____

_____

_____

_____

_____

_____

_____

_____

_____

_____

_____

_____

_____

_____

_____

_____

_____

_____

_____

_____

_____

_____

_____

_____

_____

_____

Don't be reluctant to ask questions. More people are willing to help you than you think. The sooner you realize the power of asking questions, the sooner you'll succeed. Don't drown in your pride.
~ Slim Jackson

There's so much more to being a male of color than sex and relationships. ~ Slim Jackson

There's enough food for everybody that's hungry to eat. Everybody that looks like you isn't competition. Seek to understand, then to help. In turn, people will be more willing to help you.
~ Slim Jackson

Black Men throughout history have tried to embrace their blackness through various means. They have marched, grown locks, and changed their last names to "X." In my opinion, none of these actions hold a candle to self-love you achieve through loving a black woman. That truly is the most revolutionary act.
~ Mike Phil

The act of Black Love erases all the injustices and imbalances that have shaped the black experience in this country. ~ Mike Phil

Essential Question #3

What is the best relationship you have and what makes it the best?

_____

_____

_____

_____

_____

_____

_____

_____

_____

_____

_____

_____

_____

_____

_____

_____

_____

_____

_____

_____

_____

_____

We all can love ourselves by ourselves. Black love is the only way to be able to love and understand yourself, through someone else. It's the best way to love our people in an apparent and passionate manner. ~ Mike Phil

The people we surround ourselves with typically influence how we are as individuals. ~ Alan Hamilton

As a young male of color I had to be better, faster, and smarter than my white counter-parts. Simultaneously, I had to be stronger, work harder, and tougher than my black contemporaries. ~ Fahamu Pecou

Before we can accomplish anything, we have to love ourselves. That's why it is vital that boys of color see themselves as future leaders, albeit presidents, doctors, lawyers, principals, etc. But most importantly stand up, strong men of color who are productive assets to society. ~ Wesley Bellamy

While we are competing with each other to get ahead, we have to also learn how to support and uplift each other at the same time. There is no honor in stepping on your fellow man in order to achieve success at any means necessary. ~ Senator Diallo Rabain

Essential Question #4

Which of your relationships needs the most improvement?

When you cross someone in life that you can relate to, it serves you great to boost his or her confidence level, then just maybe someone will say *"If he can do it, maybe I can too!"* ~ Senator Diallo Rabain

Culture

Everything that one becomes is due in part to environment, upbringing, and most importantly culture. The culture you live in molds how you see the world. The culture you possess molds how others see you. The things you do change your culture. How you dress. What you speak. The types of foods you eat, music you listen to, or way you carry yourself. Everything is interwoven.

Culture has already affected who you are. Mainstream culture, home culture, American culture, school culture, street culture, social media culture and Internet culture. Open your eyes, examine everything with a critical lens. Be critical of the information you let enter your system. The culture you create. The culture you consume. The culture that consumes you.

Think. Analyze. Question. Reflect. Infiltrate. Change. Evolve. Influence. Mold. Limit. Create. Your own lane. Your own identity. Your own style. Your own music. Your own system. Use this space to build your own culture.

In order to communicate with aliens, you must FIRST learn to speak their language. ~ Alfred Blake

Essentially, Hip-Hop is the most exciting cultural phenomenon to emerge in the last century. Youth are deeply involved in it, and are displaying such intellectual veracity when expressing their connection to it that it only makes sense to create opportunities for them to use it in formal educational settings.

~Dr. Christopher Emdin

The reality is, that our elders will not survive if they don't know how to speak the language of the youth. The language of the youth is Pop Culture, and our elders must accept and adapt if they truly want to reach the youth. ~ Alfred Blake

Hip-Hop connects the youth with our elders. I want our youth to know that we can have an amazing legacy and a wealth of information in our elders and that if we reach back, we can really grow as a culture and individually. ~ O'hene Savant

_____

_____

_____

_____

_____

_____

_____

_____

_____

_____

_____

_____

_____

_____

_____

_____

_____

_____

_____

_____

_____

_____

_____

_____

_____

We have an interest in public safety so we must contribute to the safety and development of crime ridden and dysfunctional neighborhoods. ~ Bruce Bryan

Essential Question #1

We are all so different in many ways. Make a list of how people are different. How can you celebrate the differences between cultures?

_____

_____

_____

_____

_____

_____

_____

_____

_____

_____

_____

_____

_____

_____

_____

_____

_____

_____

_____

_____

_____

_____

_____

_____

_____

_____

_____

_____

It is important for incarcerated people to know that where they are does not have to define who they are, nor does it determine who they become because they are not their past, they are not their mistakes.
~ Bruce Bryan

Two assets that incarcerated people have are their time and minds. Even while incarcerated they have the freedom to become better human beings and to do better. ~ Bruce Bryan

It is paramount that incarcerated people understand that they possess inalienable, redeemable qualities that they can change the way they live by changing the way they think. They can become agents of change from behind prison walls. ~ Bruce Bryan

Positive images allow us to continue raising the bar of success and model it out for those who may not have access to positive influences in their households, schools, or communities.
~ Kenny Pugh

The ability to *"code switch"* and *"wear a mask"* is a skill that I mastered early in life and has played a role in developing a dual personality that allows me to relate to street mentality as well as the politics of the American society. ~ Christopher Small

Essential Question #2

Describe an experience where you passed judgment on someone from another culture, but once you got to know the person your judgments were wrong.

We live in a complex world in which our ability to be critically aware of the things happening around us is essential to our survival and ability to thrive. ~ Charles H.F. Davis

Many of our young people never have the opportunity to discuss
how they feel or even engage in intelligent conversation.
~ Basheer Jones

Many of us have been told *"You can't!"* for so long that our minds have bought into the myth, leading us on a detour of destruction that offsets our destiny. Don't believe the myth. ~ Eddie Connor, Jr.

We need to have the tenacity of a tiger to take back our communities and the ebullience of an eagle to soar above negativity to the stratosphere of success. ~ Eddie Connor, Jr.

_____

_____

_____

_____

_____

_____

_____

_____

_____

_____

_____

_____

_____

_____

_____

_____

_____

_____

_____

_____

_____

_____

_____

_____

_____

_____

_____

_____

We can change our communities if we change the mindsets in our communities. ~ Eddie Connor, Jr.

Essential Question #3

Why is it important to embrace culture?

I say time and time again that our youth are NOT the next generation. Our youth are the NOW generation. Now is the time for our young people to dream bigger than ever before and do more than ever before. ~ Eddie Connor, Jr.

Many of our youth are hurting, coming from broken homes, seeking acceptance, and searching for their identity. There is hope and there is healing. ~ Eddie Connor, Jr.

It's time for our youth to pursue not only formal but also self-education that enriches the soul and discover their purpose, in order to manifest their destiny. ~ Eddie Connor, Jr.

Defining yourself is important, and knowing your history can be a critical piece of the puzzle. The power to define is the power to fulfill. If one cannot successfully define himself, there are outside influences that are willing to do it for him.
~ L. Trenton Marsh

How people see you determines how they act around you and determines the type of influence you have on them. ~ Alan Hamilton

Essential Question #4

How can you effectively share your culture with others?

In order to grow we have to expose ourselves to different things.
~ J.T. Solomon

Fatherhood

Parents take on a task that can never be accurately scripted, documented, or predicted. Ideally, we desire parents who are firm but tender when needed, loving, demanding, but also excellent providers of stability. Typically, mothers spark life, build compassion, nurture emotions, and an ear in times of need. Most importantly, fathers help us understand the complexities of the world, allow us to fall, but instill respect, loyalty, and dedication in our spirits. But realistically, every situation is not the same, every parent doesn't "love" the same, and every parent doesn't have to be your mother or father.

Sons*: Ask yourself, what kind of man and father would you like to be? What kind of son would you like to have? Understand that everything in life is a lesson and no one is perfect. Don't be afraid to set pride aside, ask questions, and learn as you go. Try to absorb the good from others in your life as well.*

Fathers & Future Fathers*: Be consistent and loving. Be nurturing but firm. Learn to respond instead of react. Find a routine that works for your child. Understand that neither you nor your child are perfect. Struggles bring lessons, but it is wisdom that helps us not to repeat those struggles again. Be a teacher, a guide, for what a man should be, what your son will one day be. Don't be afraid to love.*

Being a "Great" son, man, and father comes with time and wisdom. We must learn how to love others and not be afraid to love the way they need to be loved. Don't hesitate to initiate conversation. Ask "How can I love you better? When do you feel loved?" Think about these questions for yourself. Start planning your response. Put in the work now. Chase excellence.

Breaking the generational curse within my family, when it comes to fathers not being involved, is inspiring. ~ LaVar Young

_____

_____

_____

_____

_____

_____

_____

_____

_____

_____

_____

_____

_____

_____

_____

_____

_____

_____

_____

_____

_____

_____

_____

_____

_____

_____

_____

_____

_____

It is better to build a child than repair an adult. If we start when they're young then they'll be ahead of us and that's what we should want. We should want our children to be better than us.
~ Basheer Jones

Being a man isn't the alpha male images that they've been bombarded with all these years. ~ Pervis Taylor, III

I challenge my sons to do something different. My role is not to bestow self-identity on them but to expose them to things that can be used to build their identity. I teach them to feel good about taking action. My goal is to help my sons explore their uniqueness so that they can have a greater impact on the world around them. I often ask them, *"How will you impact history?"* ~ Colbert Williams

When you grow up feeling like you have missed something significant there is an evolution of thought that is required of you in order to grow past it. In doing so, we have to come to a point where we accept the things we cannot change and have the courage to change the things we can. ~ Colbert Williams

Essential Question #1

What does it mean to be a son? What does it mean to be a father or dad?

When a child experiences a new opportunity it provides them with a new lens to see the world through. But most importantly it allows them to feel good about themselves. Self-confidence, self-worth and self-esteem are all major components to ensuring that children don't become another statistic. ~ Colbert Williams

Children must be equipped with a set of principles, of values, and of morals so when they face a difficult choice or roadblock they can make a sound decision based on their personal beliefs.
~ Colbert Williams

_____
_____
_____
_____
_____
_____
_____
_____
_____
_____
_____
_____
_____
_____
_____
_____
_____
_____
_____
_____
_____
_____
_____
_____
_____
_____
_____

It is truly my belief that it takes a community to help in the rearing of children. ~ Colbert Williams

There are three things that I believe parents can do to steer their children toward a successful life. One, have a set of positive principles that your family lives by. Two, make education an important priority in your family. Finally, know that unconditional love is the key to sustaining a loving family.

~ Colbert Williams

It's okay to be scared of the unknown. I knew I was going to be a father, however, I had no idea or image that reflected that word. So I was scared and I masked that fear with shame. ~ Colbert Williams

Essential Question #2

Write a letter to your father expressing your thoughts.

_____

_____

_____

_____

_____

_____

_____

_____

_____

_____

_____

_____

_____

_____

_____

_____

_____

_____

_____

_____

_____

_____

_____

_____

_____

Own it. Accept it. Change it. Responsibility is a hard thing to understand when you are a young father. Know that the first step of being a father is first realizing that you are one. The next step is to find a father who you think is a successful one and ask him about his role. ~ Colbert Williams

Know the difference between your homeboys giving you advice and people who have been where you're headed. I learned that just because my friends were also teen fathers didn't mean that they knew *how* to be a father. ~ Colbert Williams

Part of being a father is being accountable. Effective fathers have accountability partners in their lives. Often times these partners are wives, mothers, sisters, aunts, uncles, grandparents etc. Your job will be to identify who that person is and allow them to be your support. Supportive people in your life will give you sound advice and will hold your feet to the fire so to speak when you feel like throwing in the towel. ~ Colbert Williams

You are worth more. Know that you are more than a paycheck. Your child needs support and money helps support their needs. However your love, time and presence are the gifts that will ultimately shape the life of your child(ren). My mantra is *"The best gift a father can give is his presence."* ~ Colbert Williams

Remember the old saying, *"The apple doesn't fall far from the tree?"* That means that our children do what they see us doing. An effective father understands that his behavior plays a role in the way a child sees himself. Children often do what they see and not what you say. ~ Colbert Williams

Essential Question #3

Write a letter to your son or future son expressing what you want for him.

Watch what you say. Did you know that the best weapon to use against someone is words? The first words that are heard by a child are yours. Words have power and when used out of frustration and anger they can kill self-esteem. An effective father nurtures and develops his child's self-worth and self-confidence.

~ Colbert Williams

Your word is your bond. Never say something you don't plan to
follow. An effective father keeps his word. ~ Colbert Williams

You must make a genuine and meaningful effort to reach out to your child; whether through family members, letter writing, sending drawings or post cards expressing your love and concern for them, etc. The point is to step up to the plate–as a man, and as a father. Keep a journal of all the times you've written, the times you've heard from your child and how it made you feel. If possible, keep a record of your child(ren)'s achievements. ~ Bruce Bryan

I understand that being a father is an honor and I hold my position with high esteem. The experience of fatherhood for me has been about letting go of fear, shame, past hurt, and embracing love. That's what fatherhood forces you to do; it goes against everything that people describe as being a man. ~ Colbert Williams

---

As a father, I had to learn how to communicate my feelings. I have learned to talk about my hurt, fears, and poor choices. I have even had to learn how to hug more. ~ Colbert Williams

Essential Question #4

Have you forgiven your father for any lingering pain or sorrow?

It is crucial that you let your child(ren) know that closeness is not measured by distance.~ Bruce Bryan

ADDITIONAL ESSENTIAL QUESTIONS

Education
1. List your educational goals.
2. Reading Log: Keep track of the books that you're reading and jot down a few notes about each book.
3. Make a list of things you already know and things you want to learn more about.

Spiritual
1. What do you know about different religions? Do some research to see if your understanding is correct?
2. How does your relationship with your higher power help you through your day?
3. Do you have a relationship with your higher power? Do you want to improve this relationship, if so how will you accomplish this?
4. Write a prayer that you can read and say whenever you need a little reminder of faith.
5. Do you believe your higher power has a specific blessing for you? If so, what is it?

Career Advice
1. Draw a set of stairs and plan the next few steps in your life. Come back to this whenever you need to continue planning.
2. Who has your dream career? Read his/her bio.

Advice to Young Men of Color
1. Name five people that you could go to for advice and what questions would you ask them?

Leadership
1. When have you acted as a leader?
2. Do you hold yourself accountable for your own actions?
3. What is the relationship between leaders and followers?
4. How can a leader avoid being corrupted by power?

Passion and Purpose
1. What comes naturally to you?
2. What would you do for free because you love it so much?
3. If you had 12 months to live would you still be doing what you're doing now?
4. If you had something to teach what would it be?

Words of Wisdom
1) What can you do to be wiser?
2) How do you hold yourself accountable for your actions?
3) What have been some of your experiences for speaking or acting to quickly?

Relationships
1. What have you learned from observing the relationships around you- parents, grandparents, teachers, etc.?
2. How do you build a successful and sustainable relationship with a woman?

Culture
1. Ask your parents more about your heritage. Share a story they've told you or any information you found out about your native culture.
2. How can you celebrate the differences and commonalities of those around you?

Fatherhood
1. Write a letter to fathers around the world explaining why having a relationship with your child is essential.

ABOUT BRANDON FRAME

"Be Different, Be Great, and Never Stop." is the motto that Brandon Frame not only lives by but also embodies. Hailing from Hartford, Connecticut, Brandon has always envisioned achieving his goals. As a graduate of Morehouse College, Brandon unites his passions for business and education as he creates avenues for youth to develop into positive and upstanding men and women.

His organization, TheBlackManCan has become a highly revered resource for the Black community and society as a whole. TheBlackManCan media platform is read in all 50 states and over 15 different countries. TheBlackManCan Institute has traveled to cities such as Washington D.C. Atlanta, GA, New York City, Memphis, TN and more to uplift, educate, motivate, and empower young men of color.

He currently serves as the Director of Business Partnerships and Development at High School, Inc. in his hometown. At High School, Inc., Brandon has implemented a program he designed around the motto, "Taking students from the classroom to the boardroom." It has been so successful that it is now a nationally recognized and renowned program.

Brandon is the author of the critically acclaimed interactive journal, "Define Yourself, Redefine the World: A Guided Journal for Black Men & Boys." Brandon has received numerous awards and honors, including the Excellence in Education Award from Black Street Black Celebration Awards, named Top 40 under 40 by The Hartford

Business Journal and Jet Magazine, I'm So Educated Leadership Award and the Ujima Award for Youth Involvement. Brandon is the Co-Founder of the award winning twitter chat #HipHopEd. Brandon's work has been featured in Jet Magazine, PolicyMic, Black Enterprise, The Grio, NBC New York, ABC New York and Fox Connecticut. Brandon Frame is an evolving visionary who is determined to "Be Different, Be Great, and Never Stop."

ABOUT THEBLACKMANCAN

TheBlackManCan (TBMC) is a social haven of inspiration. Founded in April 2010 by Brandon Frame, TheBlackManCan (TheBlackManCan.Org) offers a positive contradiction to the prevailing negative image of Black Men. In an age when media plays a major role in dictating our perceptions, TBMC helps to eradicate stereotypes, fight mindsets, and create a balanced mold by reinforcing that **THE BLACK MAN CAN.**

Highlighting stories in the various aspects of life for men, women, organizations, and family, TheBlackManCan is a world of its own. "Positive Black Male News" contains weekly updates on stories around the country that demonstrate or draw attention to the great things Black Men have done or are doing. TheBlackManCan highlights passion filled, successful women and men in "Exquisite Women" & "The League of Extraordinary Black Men." "The Village" recognizes organizations that have a positive impact on their surrounding communities while "Falling Black In Love" focuses on Black Love, the Black Family, and how those two aspects of life are influenced by society. All of these categories and more create a true vision of what everyone, especially young Black Men, can achieve.

TheBlackManCan is a piece of motivation for everyone. The Inaugural 2012 Black Man Can Awards honored and celebrated positive Black male role models in over ten categories. TheBlackManCan is a representation of our community and the actions of others who continue to be visionary and servant leaders. It's vital that we make it known around the world that **THE BLACK MAN CAN! Visit tbmcawards.theblackmancan.org to learn more**

TheBlackManCan Institute is a one-day mentoring Institute. TheBlackManCan Institute has traveled to New York, City, Atlanta, GA, Baltimore, MD and more to UPLIFT INSPIRE, MOTIVATE and EDUCATE boys of color. Visit **tbmcinstitute.theblackmancan.org** to learn more and see when the Institute is coming to a city near you!

BIOGRAPHIES

Akil Bello is an expert in preparing for college and graduate school prerequisite exams (SAT, LSAT, GRE, GMAT). He founded Bell Curves with his father and brother in 2003 to help provide quality test preparation and information to those in need rather than those who can most afford it.

Al Coleman is an award winning lawyer and author of *Secrets to Success: The Definitive Career Development Guide for New And First Generation Professionals.* Coleman believes in the power of mentorship and developed the Sage Pledge, a pledge mentors can take to keep them determined.

Alan Hamilton, Creative Director and owner of Original Star Media, has a strong passion and gift for art. He fully believes art is one of those things in life that helps show you anything is possible.

Alfred Blake is an entrepreneur and motivational speaker. He is the author of *The Students Handbook to Breaking All the Rules.* He is the co-founder of I am Multi L.L.C.

Alvin S. Perry, DBA, MBA is the CEO and founder of Critical Zone, Inc., (CZI). CZI helps youth and adults develop Personal Strategic Plans in support of identified life and career goals.

Andre Knighton is on a mission to share his testimony and help others. He's the CEO of God's Child Multimedia Production with a mission to assist men and women to achieve their goals through media, performing arts, and theater. He is a winner of the Inaugural Black Man Can Awards' Spirituality award.

Bahseer Jones is an acclaimed Spoken Word artist. This Morehouse graduate has received numerous accolades and honors and offers programs through The Basheer Jones Foundation.

Brandon McEachern, Founder and CEO of Broccoli City, is not afraid to go green and take his community with him. His daily motto is *"Doing what you can, with what you have, where you are."* and is focused on helping others realize their internal strengths.

Bruce Bryan is the founder of BabyDaddies2Fathers, a website geared towards inspiring and educating young men on the importance and dynamics of being a responsible, loving and proactive father. Bruce's mission is incredibly important as he targets incarcerated fathers like himself.

Cenell Harrell was the Chief Curator of Driven Magazine and is currently working on a book. He is a Sales and Marketing Professional with Living Social.

Charles H.F. Davis, III is a writer, thinker, and speaker on the rise, lending a critical voice to many social and cultural issues of our time. With a Bachelor's and two Master's degrees under his belt, Charles is currently pursuing his doctorate in Higher Education at the University of Arizona, after which he will become a college professor.

Dr. Christopher Emdin, Assistant Professor in the Department of Mathematics, Science, and Technology at Teachers College of Columbia University, is a skilled researcher, educator, and writer. He fuses Urban Education, Hip-Hop, and science into his lectures crediting their similarities and connections.

Principal at Springwood Elementary School in Tallahassee, FL, Christopher Small is an accomplished educational administrator with a passion for assisting at risk youth. He believes it's vital that educational settings help build character, integrate technology, and provide leadership opportunities for youth.

Colbert Williams is the founder of The Evolution of a Son to a Father, which aims to help men realize their value as sons and their worth as fathers to their offspring. Williams provides an array of workshops centered around developing African American males.

Darryl Baynes prides himself in "Edutainment" as he is the founder and president of Interactive Science Programs (ISP). Based out of Virginia, he recently finished the Dream Tour that provided motivational STEM programs around the country.

Darryl Frierson, writer and progressive philosopher, is the founder of the award winning blog From Ashy to Classy. Frierson is a "Normal Brother on a Road to Extraordinary Things" and describes his writing as provocative, balanced, and informative.

David McGhee is an award winning mentor, speaker, writer, college instructor, and former program director at Big Brothers Big Sisters.

Dennis Upkins is an author, freelance artist, and digital photographer in Tennessee. His love for reading and writing started at an early age and has been progressing ever since.

Convicted with the concept that one can be a positive contribution to their surroundings, Senator Diallo Rabain decided to run for Parliament in Bermuda. He enjoyed canvasing communities so he can hear directly from his constituents.

Eddie Connor, Jr.'s list of titles includes author, educator, Evangelist, motivational speaker, poet, and Radio and TV Host. His current project is CBS & CW50's "Street Beat" which focuses on injecting positivity into the lives of Detroit.

Eric Tillman is an educator and founder of Advancing Youth Minds (AYM), which assist students in overcoming obstacles to achieve their highest reach. Tillman is determined to prepare students and push them to AYM (aim) for greatness through academics and life skills.

With an affinity for art like no other, Fahamu Pccou mixes modern issues with hip hop culture using bright colors, and an evolving promotional campaign. Pecou has received a long list of awards and recognition from some of the most premier institutions, publications, and museums.

Author, brand specialist, consultant, entrepreneur, and keynote speaker, George A. Olokun is driven. His book, *Empowered to Achieve: 50 Keys to Being & Becoming*, is a guide created to help motivate others.

Howard R. Jean is the Founder and CEO of S.E.I.L (Success through Education, Inspiration and Leadership), which provides support and resources to members of the community through programs and mentorship.

Photographer Ivory Lawrence lusts to create picture perfect moments of frozen time. His business, Alter Ego Photography highlights the multiple personalities individuals possess and showcases them with photographical art.

J. Newry is an influential and upcoming gospel artist. He started music at an early age. At 17, he directed, arranged, and orchestrated an original composition to a 200+ choir and released his debut CD *The Beginning.*

With a passion to create meaningful projects that inspire and uplift, James Bland is a multi-talented actor and filmmaker who executive produces and stars in the hit comedy series FAIL. He has written and directed multiple films including *Cocoa Love*, a romantic comedy that has aired on both BET and the ASPiRE network. Currently, James is producing the psychological thriller, *The Hypnotist*, which was recently named a NBC Short Cuts finalist.

Dr. James L. Moore, III is an educator, counselor and author. He recently released his book *African American Students in Urban Schools* and is the Director of the Todd Anthony Bell National Resource Center on the African American Male and Associate Provost at Ohio State University.

Jarret Janako is a bicoastal actor from Philly who has been seen in several TV shows, films, commercials, and music videos. Some of his work includes Law and Order and a lead role in artist Monica's "Until its Gone." He's a graduate of Temple University holding a B.A in Theatre and Public Relations.

Founder of Empowering Ourselves, Jarrett Mathis is an inspirational leader in his community. He advocates for self-respect, eliminating the use of the n-word, and eradicating other negative influences. He seeks to find ways to empower youth.

272

Brother Jesse Muhammad is an award winning blogger, writer for *The Final Call*, experienced community organizer, and touring national motivational speaker. His motivational theme is "Mediocrity is Not in Your D.N.A."

John Phillip Autry, II has a passion for acting and doesn't allow being born deaf/hard of hearing to stop him from pursuing his dreams. John serves on the board of No Limit and helps many young deaf children enhance their communication and auditory skills and reach their goals.

Founder of F.I.R.M magazine, J.T. Solomon's dream of having his own magazine came full circle after being laid off in 2009. J.T. was able to launch the magazine, which focuses on Fashion, Investment, Recreation, and Music (F.I.R.M). J.T. is an 8th grade English Language Arts Teacher at The Eagle Academy for Young Men at Ocean Hill in Brooklyn, NY.

Julian Streete is the founder and creator of JStreet Branding, an Atlanta based graphic design and branding company. Like good design, JStreet Branding's process is simple: *Dream, Design, Deliver.*

Karl-Edwin Guerre has been featured in GQ Japan, Arise Magazine, Essence, Vogue Italy/Vogue Black, and on Details.com. His website, Guerreisms.com has been showcasing fashion and style for several years.

Keishorne Scott is co-founder of the Be Positive Campaign. Their latest initiative is the "One More Educated Black Man" project. Keishorne is the author the inspirational bestseller *L.I.F.E. Love Insecurities, Friends and Envy.*

Kel Spencer is known as The Warrior Poet and The Fresh Prince of Brooklyn. Kel is an emerging Indie Hip-Hop Artist, award-winning songwriter, and poet. He's also the founder of the Pens of Power Program that promotes writing with an urban twist to engage youth.

Kenny Pugh is known as The Life & Relationship Strategist. Kenny Pugh is also a bestselling author, minister, and radio personality. The mission of his business, Kenny Pugh L.L.C., is to help people transform their lives through life-changing events, radio, television, and multi-media resources.

Kevin Ollie is the Head Coach of the University of Connecticut Men's Basketball team. He speaks to youth about the importance of being a scholar athlete and obtaining your college degree.

Author of *"From 1.0 to 4.0,"* L. Trenton Marsh shares his experience with time management throughout out his academic career. Entrepreneur, public speaker, and scholar, L. Trenton March was the first African-American male student commencement speaker at George Washington University.

The President and CEO of Newark Now, LaVar Young pushes men to become better men and engaging fathers. He says economic stability, empowerment, and encouragement are necessary to help someone become a better parent.

Marcus Singletary transformed his life by defying low academics in high school, pushing to obtain his GED and later graduate college. Marcus advocates for the importance of being a scholar-athlete and maintaining balance, using his own story for motivation.

Matthew Smith believes that "Together we can fill the cup of childhood creativity." He's the Executive Director of Building Better Futures and Matt's Music. His passion for musical instruments has opened doors throughout his life.

Mike Mose is the author of *One Drop Too White* that covers self-acceptance for black men. Mike aims to educate and entertain his readers with positive, realistic images of black people.

Mike Phil is a liberal, post racist, Agnostic, pro-feminist. He believes common sense is a refusal to individually reason and would be a proactive Darwinist if permitted.

Rapper, producer, and multi-instrumentalist O'hene Savant is the founding member, owner, and first artist of Rham Nation LLC, Soul Model Records, and Savant Clothing. O'hene is a well-rounded artist with a Neo-Cubism cultural background infused into everything he does.

Omarr Lee's life experiences showcase the true definition of possessing faith and perseverance. Just before graduating high school as a star athlete, he was involved in a car accident and suffered a traumatic brain injury. He defied the prognosis and counsels youth on the importance of spiritual foundation and believing in oneself.

Orayne Williams is the founder of D.R.E.A.M Inc., (Dispelling Realities & Empowering African-America Minds Inc.) which aims to educate and motivate urban youth in financial literacy. Orayne leads workshops on understanding financial basics, credit, and money management.

Paul Wilson, Jr. is a marketplace minister, author, and speaker who is *"Igniting exponential ideas to create extraordinary lives!"* He has an expertise in marketplace ministry, youth development, entrepreneurship, and uniting it all together.

Pervis Taylor, III is a contributor to Vibe Vixen Magazine and Crossroads Magazine. He's committed to empowering a generation of young people, particularly young Black men, to realize their purpose.

Rahfeal Gordon went from homeless in New Jersey to published CEO and motivational speaker. He tours the country promoting his work and speaking via his businesses RahGor Motivations & Publishing.

Dr. Raymond Hicks served as the 5th president of his alma mater, Grambling State University. In addition, he was behind the nationally recognized service-learning program, Alliances for Community Development, designed to increase the personal aspirations of Black boys.

Renard Antonio Green's passion for financial, marketing, and project management fuels The R2 Consulting Group in which he is President and CEO. He is the recipient of the Pacesetter Award by the Ohio State University Max. M. Fisher College of Business that honored his academics, leadership skills, and community service.

Ricardo Deveaux is a community activist, motivational speaker, and visionary leader in the Bahamas. He's currently the President and CEO of the Bahamas Primary School Student of the Year Foundation and the leader behind Vision 2 Lead.

Slim Jackson is Executive Editor & CEO at popular blog, Single Black Male. Freelance Writer. He's a lover of personal development, entrepreneurship, laughter, and life.

Terrell Hill is the founding principal of High School, Inc. in Hartford, CT. He is leading the charge to make it a national school of excellence. Terrell is a servant leader with a passion for education, finance, and leadership.

Founder of One Black Man, Tim Lee is a teacher, motivational speaker, preacher, and mentor. One Black Man is his non-profit that seeks to encourage, enlighten, and inspire African American males between the ages of 13 to 18 with programs that focus on leadership, self-esteem, and more.

Vensin Gray has a passion for writing infused with his concepts of faith and God. He is the author of *The ProChrist* and currently working on his next book.

Dr. Walter Kimbrough is the former President of Philander Smith College. He is currently Dillard University's 7th President. Dr. Kimbrough has a long list of accolades that highlight his passions for education, fraternity, and revitalization of everything he touches.

Wayne Smith is the Mayor of Irvington, New Jersey and was elected for an unprecedented 3rd term in 2010. He advocates for youth to be community leaders and take control of the world you wish to see.

Founder of Helping Young People Evolve (H.Y.P.E), Wesley Bellamy is committed to education and youth development. His non-profit aims to establish discipline, organization, and support for youth during after school programs.

CONTACT INFORMATION

Brandon Frame
Chief Visionary Officer
TheBlackManCan
www.theblackmancan.org
Twitter: @TheBlackManCan
Facebook: The Black Man Can
Email: Brandon.m.frame@gmail.com

Julian Streete
Founder & Creative Director
JStreet Branding
www.jstreetbranding.com
Twitter: @JStreetBranding
Facebook: /jstreetbranding
Email: julian@jstreetbranding.com

JoVonna Rodriguez
Owners & Editor
Literacy Lives LLC
www.literacylives.com
Facebook: /LiteracyLives
Email: LiteracyLives@yahoo.com

30015579R00162

Made in the USA
Middletown, DE
10 March 2016